Sandra Beale

Series editor
DR ALISTAIR BRYCE-CLEGG

50 fantastic ideas for STEM activities

BLOOMSBURY

BLOOMSBURY EDUCATION
Bloomsbury Publishing Plc
50 Bedford Square, London, WC1B 3DP, UK
29 Earlsfort Terrace, Dublin 2, Ireland

BLOOMSBURY, BLOOMSBURY EDUCATION and the Diana logo are trademarks of Bloomsbury Publishing Plc
First published in Great Britain, 2025 by Bloomsbury Publishing Plc
This edition published in Great Britain, 2025 by Bloomsbury Publishing Plc

Text copyright © Sandra Beale, 2025
Photographs © Sandra Beale, 2025 / Laura Neate, 2025 / Shutterstock, 2025

Sandra Beale has asserted her right under the Copyright, Designs and Patents Act, 1988,
to be identified as Author of this work

Bloomsbury Publishing Plc does not have any control over, or responsibility for,
any third-party websites referred to or in this book. All internet addresses given in this book
were correct at the time of going to press. The author and publisher regret any inconvenience
caused if addresses have changed or sites have ceased to exist, but can accept no responsibility
for any such changes

All rights reserved. No part of this publication may be reproduced or transmitted in any form or by
any means, electronic or mechanical, including photocopying, recording, or any information storage
or retrieval system, without prior permission in writing from the publishers

A catalogue record for this book is available from the British Library

ISBN: PB: 978-1-8019-9617-4; ePDF: 978-1-8019-9614-3

2 4 6 8 10 9 7 5 3 1 (paperback)

Design concept by Lynda Murray
Text design by Laura Neate

Printed and bound in India by Thomson Press (India) Ltd.

To find out more about our authors and books visit www.bloomsbury.com and sign up for our newsletters

Acknowledgements:
I would like to dedicate this book to my three children Charlie, Oliver and Amelie who were my
inspiration for my toddler and Early Years STEM sessions. I would also like to acknowledge
my scientist husband Mathew. I would also like to thank and acknowledge the wonderful parents and
their marvellous children who have come to all of my in-person and online sessions over the last 10 years.
It is their participation which makes my STEM sessions so special.

Contents

Introduction 4

Gases
Climbing water 6
Dancing bells 7
Self-inflating balloons 8
Water fountains 10
Air in a bottle 11
Rainbow volcano 12

Materials
Making snow 14
Balloon kebabs 15
Bouncing marble 16
Art with shaving foam and bubble wrap 18
Painting on ice 19
Layers of the Earth 20

Forces
Static electricity 22
Magnetic suspension 23
Electromagnets 24
Lifting a jar of rice with a pencil 25
Finding the centre of gravity 26
Creating craters 27
Newton's tumbling beads 28

Water
The shape of water 29
Electrolysis 30
Travelling water 32
Floating water 33
Sticks through bags of water 34
Rescuing toys trapped in ice 35

Lava lamp 36
Buoyancy 38

The human body
Sneezing noses 39
Pumping lungs 40
Exploring sound 42
Layers of the skin 43
Pumping hearts 44
Composition of blood 46

Engineering
Making a working well 47
Making a working catapult 48
Building with paper 49
Making a conveyor belt 50
Making a maze 52

Colour and light
Sundial 53
Painting coloured shadows 54
Colouring water with light......................... 55
Capillary rainbows 56
Making rainbows outside 57
Outlining shadows 58
Light refraction with three glasses 59

Motion and movement
Painting with marbles 60
Hovercraft 61
See-saw candle 62
Newton's theory of motion with coins 63
Making a zip wire 64

Introduction

Asking questions about how the world works is a crucial part of childhood development and fundamental to this understanding is Science, Technology, Engineering and Maths (STEM). A further component of this is Art (STEAM), which encourages creativity and the ability to think out of the box.

I started teaching basic STEM concepts to my nine-month-old son nearly 10 years ago and was amazed at how engaged he was. Visiting friends were fascinated to see a baby performing science experiments and wanted their own children to participate. I started hosting groups of preschool children and their parents in my kitchen every week, and we explored exciting colours, fizzes and pops. This became a regular event, offered to my local community for free. The sessions moved online in 2020 during the early stages of the Covid-19 pandemic, opening my work to a broader audience around the UK and internationally.

My sessions are very child-led and the children have the freedom to play and explore while doing the activities, all within a safe environment. I believe there is no right or wrong way to reach a conclusion. It is important to take different approaches, which encourages the children to think 'out of the box' and promotes independent thinking in the future.

This book provides practitioners, teachers, carers and parents with 50 easy and stimulating activities to do with their young charges, using simple items and materials that can be found in every nursery, home or Early Years setting. These are adaptable and can be carried out with very young children, from about nine months to older children in preschool and reception. In a busy setting, it is advisable to carry out the activities in small groups with at least one or more adults present.

All the activities have been tried and tested with the children who come to my weekly STEM sessions. Quite often the children themselves take the concept and turn it into something else, which I generally find works much better. At my sessions, the children learn to work individually as well as in a team. They develop the ability to think creatively and come up with clever and interesting solutions.

The activities in this book are designed to allow young children to play and have fun through discovery and exploration, which aids their learning process. They are designed to encourage young children to develop their language, vocabulary and communication skills through asking questions and discussing what they see. The activities also aim to support the children's understanding of the world, physical development and mathematical, literacy and expressive art and design skills.

The main purpose of this book is to make STEM (or STEAM) fun and exciting for both the children and adults involved. I believe that STEM is vital to us as a nation. The 0–6 age group are at the most curious of all stages; encouraging them to ask and investigate questions that interest them fulfils that natural inquisitiveness. We are surrounded by science; it is all around us and we must never be afraid of it.

Instead, let's embrace it as young children do – with joy, passion and curiosity.

Health and Safety

All activities must be supervised by an adult. Children must never be left alone when doing these activities. Always explain to the children about the materials and equipment that they will be using, and make sure that if using fire they understand that they must never touch it but watch from a safe distance.

How to use this book

The pages are all organised in the same way. Before you start any activity, read through everything on the page so that you are familiar with the whole activity and what you might need to plan in advance.

What you need lists the resources required for the activity. These are likely to be readily available in most settings or can be bought or made easily.

What to do tells you step-by-step what you need to do to complete the activity.

Top tips are helpful hints to make an activity work well and have been learned from experience!

The **Health & Safety tips** are often obvious, but safety cannot be overstressed. In many cases, there are no specific hazards involved in completing the activity, and your usual health and safety measure should be enough. In others, there are particular issues to be noted and addressed.

Taking it forward gives ideas for additional activities on the same theme, or for developing the activity further. These will be particularly useful for things that have gone especially well or where children show a real interest. In many cases they use the same resources, and in every case they have been designed to extend learning and broaden the children's experiences.

What's in it for the children? tells you (and others) briefly how the suggested activities contribute to learning.

Videos of some of the activities are available to download via the QR codes in the text or from the Bloomsbury Education 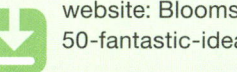 website: Bloomsbury.pub/50-fantastic-ideas-stem

Climbing water
Exploring fire and air pressure

What you need:
- Plates (ceramic or porcelain)
- Food colouring
- Tea lights
- Matches or lighter
- Water
- Glasses

What to do:
1. Gather the children and ask them what they know about fire. Discuss their answers. Explain to the children that a flame needs air to burn.
2. Ask the children to squirt a drop of different food colouring onto the plate.
3. Put a lit tea light in the middle of the plate and pour the water around it without wetting the wick.
4. Put the glass over the tea light. Ask the children to watch what happens to the tea light, the food colouring and the water on the plate. Putting a glass over the flame removes the air and pulls up the water from the plate whilst mixing the colours.
5. Discuss the children's observations.

What's in it for the children?
The children learn that fire needs air to burn. This activity is a visual way for them to understand the scientific concept and make links between what they see in front of them with what they already know about fire.

Taking it forward
- Use this activity as part of a topic on firefighters: arrange for a firefighter to come into the setting and talk about how they put out fires.

 Health & Safety
Carefully supervise children around an open flame.

Top tip
Try using two different colours on the plate (e.g. blue and yellow) to reinforce colour mixing.

 Scan the QR code to see a video of this activity.

Dancing bells
Learning how bubbles make bells move

What you need:
- Glasses or vases
- 4–5 bells (small or medium) or one small cup of dry rice per child
- Clear lemonade or tonic water

What to do:
1. Gather the children and discuss with them what they already know about bubbles and fizzy drinks.
2. Provide each child with a glass or vase or ask them to share.
3. Give each child four to five bells or a small cup of dry rice.
4. Pour the lemonade into the glasses or vases.
5. Ask the children to drop in the bells or the rice.
6. Ask the children to watch the bells or the rice moving in the liquid and then discuss what they think is happening and why.
7. Explain to them that carbon dioxide (i.e. the bubbles) attaches to the bells and lifts them up to the surface. When the bubbles pop the bells will make a jingling sound.

What's in it for the children?
The children learn that carbon dioxide is what causes bubbles in fizzy drinks. Discussing what they can see and making links to the world around them develops their communication and language skills.

Taking it forward
- Use popcorn instead of bells or rice. Ask the children to observe what might be different.
- Use different types of fizzing tablets in different glasses of tap water and compare them to the lemonade. Ask the children which glass they think might have the faster bubbles and why.

Top tip
Use uncooked rice if you do not have access to bells. If using bells, link this activity to learning about musical instruments or the Christmas song 'Jingle Bells'.

Self-inflating balloons
Learning about gases and reactions

What you need:
- Plastic bottles (1.5 litres, one per child)
- Balloons (one per child)
- A measuring jug
- White vinegar (250 ml per child)
- Food colouring
- Funnels
- Bicarbonate of soda

What to do:
1. Ask the children to sit around a table. Ask them what they know about balloons and how they are blown up.
2. Give each child a plastic bottle and a balloon or ask them to share and take turns.
3. Show the children the vinegar, ask them to smell it and guess what it might be. Relate it to their prior knowledge of crisp flavours or what they might put on fish and chips.
4. Measure 250 ml of vinegar and pour it into the bottles.
5. Ask the children to squeeze two drops of food colouring into their bottles.
6. Using the funnel, spoon two teaspoons of bicarbonate of soda into the balloon.
7. Put the balloon over the mouth of the bottle and gently tap it.
8. Ask the children to watch the balloon as it inflates.
9. Ask the children what they think might be happening.
10. Explain to them (once they have responded) that an invisible gas known as carbon dioxide is created when bicarb and vinegar come together. This causes the balloon to inflate.

What's in it for the children?

In this fun and visual activity, the children learn how bicarbonate and vinegar combine to form a gas which can inflate a balloon without the use of a pump. Making predictions, discussing their observations and taking turns will help their communication and language skills.

Taking it forward

- Experiment with using different amounts of bicarbonate and vinegar in different bottle sizes.
- Discuss with the children what effect they think this will have and record their observations.

 Scan the QR code to see a video of this activity.

50 fantastic ideas for STEM

Water fountains
Exploring air pressure

What you need:
- Plastic bottles (1.5 litres)
- Balloons
- Bendy straws
- Scissors
- Sticky tack or plasticine
- Jugs
- Water
- Food colouring
- Balloon pump (optional)
- Bowls

Top tip
Add food colouring to the water to make it easier to see.

What's in it for the children?
Through this activity the children learn about air pressure and force. They will see how the invisible air in the balloon is strong enough to push water out of a bottle through a straw. They can relate this new knowledge to things they already know about water fountains.

Taking it forward
- Ask the children what would happen if you made multiple holes in the bottle or attached three half-full bottles together with straws, with balloons over the top of the bottles.

 Scan the QR code to see a video of this activity.

What to do:
1. Gather the children and explain to them that they are going to make water fountains. Ask them what they think a water fountain might be and if they have seen one before. Ask them how they think a water fountain might work. Explain to the children that this water fountain will look different to the ones they have seen but they both use air pressure.
2. Give each child a 1.5 litre plastic bottle, a balloon and straw or tell them to share.
3. Using scissors (adults only), make a small hole in the middle of the bottle.
4. Push the long part of the straw through the hole. Make sure the bendy part of the straw is sticking outwards of the bottle and facing downwards like a tap.
5. Seal around the hole with sticky tack or plasticine.
6. Fill the jug with water and ask each child to put in a drop of food colouring. Help the children to pour the water into their bottles.
7. Blow or pump up the balloon and then put it over the top of the bottle without tying a knot in it.
8. Position the bowl under the straw.
9. Ask the children to watch what happens to the water once the air from the balloon goes into the bottle.
10. Explain to the children that the air from the balloon is being forcefully pushed into the bottle, thus pushing the water out through the straw.

Air in a bottle
Understanding that air takes up space

What you need:
- Plastic bottles (1.5 litres)
- Balloons
- Scissors
- Funnels
- Food colouring
- Jugs
- Water

What to do:
1. Gather the children and talk to them about the air around them. Ask them what they know about air and if air can be seen.
2. Give each child an empty plastic bottle or get them to share.
3. Show them the bottle. Ask them to look inside and turn it upside down. Tell them that the bottle is full of air.
4. Cut the neck off a balloon and put it over the bottom of the funnel so that part of the balloon neck sticks down into the bottle and an airtight seal is created.
5. Ask the children what they think might happen when the water goes into the funnel.
6. Put some food colouring into a jug of water. Let the children take turns pouring the water very quickly into the funnel.
7. The water should trickle into the bottle but most of it should sit in the funnel, demonstrating that the air in the bottle is preventing the water from gushing in.

Top tip
It may take several tries of adjusting the seal to enable this activity to work the way it should.

What's in it for the children?
The children learn that air is everywhere even though they cannot see it. They also develop their communication, teamwork and turn-taking skills.

Taking it forward
- Show the children that if air is squeezed out of the bottle, then some of the water in the funnel will go into the bottle.
- Ask them to look at the top of the funnel when the bottle is squeezed and see the bubbles the air makes in the water.

 Scan the QR code to see a video of this activity.

Rainbow volcano
Watching reactions and eruptions

What you need:
- Plastic test tubes (one per child)
- Teaspoons
- Bicarbonate of soda
- Food colouring (rainbow colours)
- Vinegar
- Bowls or small containers
- Pipettes (one per child)

What to do:
1. Gather the children and ask them what they know about volcanoes. Show them videos of volcanoes erupting.
2. Give each child a test tube or ask them to share.
3. Spoon two heaped teaspoons of bicarbonate of soda into each test tube.
4. Give each child a different colour of food colouring and ask the children to squirt a few drops into their test tube.
5. Pour some vinegar into the bowls.
6. Hand out pipettes to each child. Then ask them to pull up the vinegar into the pipette by squeezing the soft top and to release the vinegar into the test tube.
7. After a few times of releasing vinegar into the bicarb, the volcano will start to bubble up over the rim of the test tube and run down the side.
8. Ask the children to discuss what might be happening. Explain to them that the bicarb and vinegar are causing a chemical reaction and is creating the bubbles to grow and 'erupt' out of the test tube.

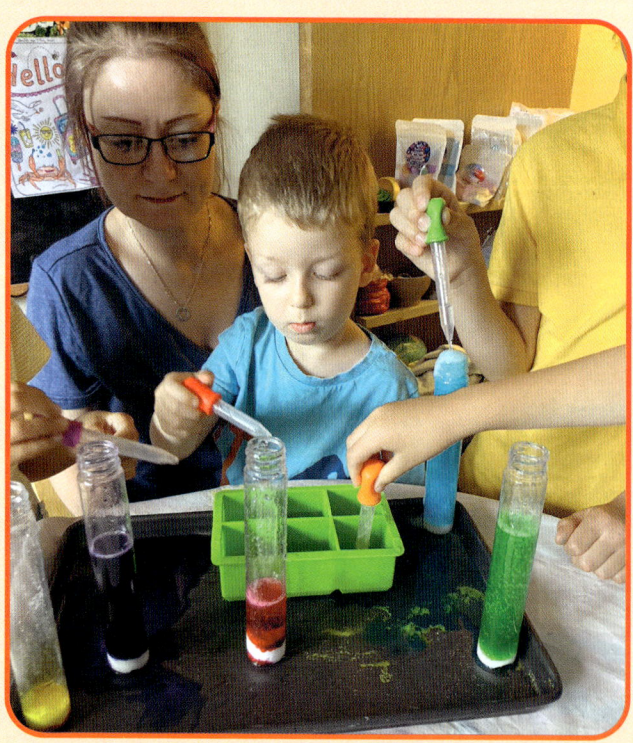

What's in it for the children?

This activity builds a sense of awe and wonder in the children, sparking their curiosity and linking what they see to their understanding of the world. Using pipettes helps to build hand strength and develop fine motor skills.

Taking it forward

- Mix bicarbonate of soda and poster paint together. Get the children to sprinkle the mixture onto paper then ask them to squirt vinegar over it to make a 'fizzy painting'.

- Create a vibrant wall display of the children's 'fizzy paintings' alongside what they have learned about volcanoes.

Top tip ⭐

Use biodegradeable glitter or sequins to make the activity more visually exciting. Adding a drop of washing up liquid to the mix will make it frothier.

Scan the QR code to see a video of this activity.

Making snow
A fun winter-themed activity

What you need:
- Large trays
- Shaving foam
- Bicarbonate of soda
- Arts and crafts supplies (for example, coloured card pipe cleaners, googly eyes)
- Small toys (dolls, toy houses, cars and so on)

What to do:
1. Gather the children and ask them what they know about snow and explain that they will be making their own version from two simple ingredients.
2. Squirt a large dollop of shaving foam onto the tray and then spoon in two or three large spoonfuls of bicarbonate of soda.
3. Mix until you get a snow-like consistency. Test it by making a ball and add more bicarbonate of soda or shaving foam as needed.
4. Discuss with the children what they see is happening.
5. Allow the children to play with the snow, making snow men and snowballs.
6. Provide the children with toys and craft supplies so that they can create their own winter scene.

What's in it for the children?
The children will see how the bicarbonate of soda reacts with the shaving foam to make a snow-like texture. Linking the activity to what they know about winter helps to develop the children's communication skills as well as their understanding of the world.

Taking it forward
- Encourage the children to use their winter scenes as part of small world play.
- Develop literacy skills by writing a story together about winter.
- Display pictures of the children's winter scenes alongside vocabulary about winter.

Top tip
Add a few drops of peppermint oil to the snow and include pine needles and pinecones if you have some.

Balloon kebabs
Testing the elasticity of a balloon

What you need:
- Balloons
- Balloon pump (optional)
- Wooden skewers

What to do:
1. Give the children an uninflated balloon each and give them a chance to explore.
2. Introduce new vocabulary: stretchy, rubber and polymers (substance made of long chains of tiny things called molecules). Discuss with the children what they think the words might mean.
3. Explain to the children that you will be pushing a skewer through a balloon without popping it.
4. Blow up a balloon, tie a knot in it and show the children that the rubber next to the knot and at the top of the balloon are quite thick and not stretched, unlike the rest of the balloon.
5. Slowly push the pointy end of the skewer through the thick part of the balloon (next to the knot) and out of the top of the balloon.
6. Explain to the children that balloon rubber stretches when the skewer is pushed through and then closes back over it.

What's in it for the children?
The children will learn that balloons are stretchy and will communicate their ideas about different materials with each other. They will marvel at how the balloon doesn't pop when the skewer goes in and ask questions to find out why.

Taking it forward
- Use different size balloons and ask the children to predict how many small balloons could go on the same skewer without popping.

Top tip
Do not blow the balloon up too big or too small as this will make it harder to push the skewer through. Provide ear defenders for children who don't like loud noises.

Health & Safety
Always supervise children carefully when using skewers.

Bouncing marble
Testing how high a marble can bounce

What you need:
- Marbles or pom poms
- Balloons
- Scissors
- Drinking glasses or cups

⊕ Health & Safety
Supervise the children carefully around marbles and make sure they do not put them in their mouths. Replace the marbles with pom poms for children under three.

What to do:
1. Gather the children and ask them if they think a marble can bounce. Let them try bouncing marbles on the table or floor. Ask them to discuss their observations.
2. Show them some uninflated balloons and give them a chance to stretch them. Explain that you will show them how to bounce a marble on a balloon.
3. Cut the neck off the balloon and stretch the body over the top of a glass making sure there are no bubbles or dimples in the balloon. It must be a smooth and taut surface.
4. Ask the children to take turns dropping marbles in the centre of the balloon.
5. Ask them to discuss their observations. They might need to practise before they get it right.
6. Explain to the children that, although the marble is hard, the stretched balloon is elastic and therefore it can change shape when the marble is dropped on it. The balloon then regains its shape when the marble bounces upwards, like a trampoline.

Scan the QR code to see a video of this activity.

What's in it for the children?

The children learn that marbles can bounce up and down on a stretchy surface. This is because the balloon is elastic and it changes shape when the marble is dropped on it but regains its shape when the marble bounces upwards.

Taking it forward

- Use different sized marbles and glasses and ask the children to predict what might happen.

- Extend the children's listening skills by asking if the marble sounds different when it's bouncing on an empty glass as compared to a glass full of water.

- Develop the children's counting skills by asking them to count how many times the marble bounces before falling off.

- Try using a range of different materials (such as paper, felt or cloth) and ask the children to discuss why the marble doesn't bounce in the same way.

Top tip ⭐

Make sure the marble is dropped in the centre of the stretched balloon, and that the balloon is stretched taut across the glass and does not have any dimples.

Art with shaving foam and bubble wrap
Expressive art using different materials

What you need:
- Bubble wrap
- Shaving foam (not gel)
- Food colouring or paint
- Sheets of white paper
- Wooden spatulas (optional)

What to do:
1. Give each child an A4 piece of bubble wrap and squirt shaving foam on the bubble side.
2. Ask the children to squirt drops of different coloured food colouring or paint onto the shaving foam.
3. Ask the children to flip the bubble wrap over onto an A4 sheet of white paper and with their fingers to press down on all the bubbles. The children can use wooden spatulas if they prefer.
4. Once the bubbles have been popped, ask the children to carefully remove the bubble wrap from the paper.
5. Ask the children to observe the pattern that the bubble wrap has made on the paper and discuss how it was made.

What's in it for the children?
This activity helps the children to understand the difference between materials and encourages them to explore different textures. It encourages them to make their own choices, create expressive art and explore colour and colour mixing.

Taking it forward
- Link this activity with maths learning: can the children use different colours to make a repeating pattern?
- Test different materials such as sand and paint instead of shaving foam and ask the children to observe the results.
- Make a link with outdoor learning: use leaves instead of bubble wrap to see the different patterns that they make.

Top tip
Give the children an A4 sheet of white paper and cut an A4 size of bubble wrap for the best effects.

Painting on ice
Learning about melting and freezing

What you need:
- Trays
- Ice
- Paintbrushes
- Paint
- Salt
- Paper

Top tip
Ice trays can be bought cheaply online – use different shapes and sizes for added fun!

What to do:
1. Put a few trays of different sizes or shapes of ice cubes in front of the children. Ask them what they know about ice and introduce the concepts of melting and freezing.
2. Ask the children to feel the sticky texture of the ice.
3. Give the children some paintbrushes and pots of paint and ask them to paint on the ice. Take pictures of the children's ice paintings before they melt.
4. Ask the children what might happen to the ice if you sprinkled some salt on the ice.
5. Explain to the children that the salt breaks the ice so cracks appear in the ice. You could discuss how salt or grit is used on the road when it's icy.
6. Encourage the children to touch the ice after you have sprinkled salt on it and ask them to describe what they can feel. Ask them to look at how their paint appears to seep into the ice through the cracks.

What's in it for the children?
The children learn about how water freezes to turn into ice. They also learn cause and effect when the salt melts the ice and changes the patterns of their ice paintings.

Taking it forward
- Once the ice has melted, ask the children to dip a piece of paper into the tray to see what different patterns come out.

50 fantastic ideas for STEM

Layers of the Earth
Understanding the planet we live on

What you need:

- Play dough in the following colours:
  - Red
  - Orange
  - Yellow
  - Black
  - Brown
  - Blue
  - Green
- Plastic knife or ruler

What to do:

1. Gather the children and explain to them that they will be creating the layers of the Earth. Ask them if they know how many layers the earth might have. Discuss their answers and explain that the Earth has seven layers.

2. To demonstrate: take a small amount of red play dough, roll it into a ball and explain that at the centre of the Earth lies the core which is very hot.

3. Around the core is the outer core which is orange. Take a bit of the orange play dough and flatten it out with your palm and put it over the core.

4. Take some yellow play dough and explain to the children that it's the mantle of the Earth, flatten it out and put it over the outer core.

5. Then take the black play dough and explain that it's the crust of the Earth and is very hard.

6. Flatten out the brown play dough for the soil, blue for the seas, then add the green for the land and trees.

7. Give each child bits of play dough and let them create their 'Earth', explaining and counting the layers as they go.

8. Once they have finished, help them cut their 'Earth' in half so that all the layers are seen clearly.

Scan the QR code to see a video of this activity.

What's in it for the children?

The children are introduced to new vocabulary: core, mantle and crust. They develop their understanding of the world around them and improve their hand strength and fine motor skills from manipulating the play dough.

Taking it forward

- This activity works well as part of a topic on the planets.
- Develop the children's understanding of the planets further by getting them to make their own solar systems.

Static electricity
Learning about electric charges

What you need:
- Balloons
- A balloon pump (optional)
- Tissue paper
- Scissors

What's in it for the children?
The children learn about static electricity and explore different forces they can feel. Discussing their observations helps to develop their communication and language skills.

Taking it forward
- Ask the children to try out different materials to create static electricity. For example, turn on a tap and ask the children to rub a ruler on their hair. Hold it near the water to see what happens.

What to do:
1. Gather the children and ask them if they know what static electricity means.
2. Discuss their answers and then explain that static electricity is caused by rubbing an object on hair or on a furry jumper. Explain that when a balloon is rubbed on hair something called electrons are added to the balloon and these are negatively charged.
3. Demonstrate this by rubbing a balloon on your hair and then gently holding the balloon over a a small piece of tissue paper to make it stand or flutter. When the balloon touches the paper it lifts it, because the paper is positively charged and opposite charges are attracted to each other.
4. Give each child a blown-up balloon and let them choose a tissue paper shape to try out the activity.
5. Encourage the children to make their own discoveries. Ask them to talk to each other about what they have noticed.

Top tip
Prepare this activity ahead of time by pumping the balloons up and cutting out shapes in tissue paper.

Magnetic suspension
Exploring magnetic fields

What you need:
- Magnetic wands or large magnets (one per child)
- Ruler
- Scissors
- Sticky tape
- Paper clips or bells

What to do:
1. Gather the children and give them a range of magnets and some time to explore them. Ask them what they already know about magnets and introduce the words attract and repel.
2. Use the ruler and scissors to measure and cut 30cm of thread.
3. Stick one end of the thread to the table with the sticky tape.
4. Tie a paper clip or bell to the other end of the thread.
5. Ask the children to lift the paper clip with the magnet and to gently pull the magnet up so that the paper clip hovers in midair.
6. You can ask the children to slip a finger between the magnet and the paper clip.
7. Explain that the paper clip is suspended in the magnetic field created by the magnet. The stronger that the magnet is, the stronger the force field will be.

What's in it for the children?
The children will learn about magnetic fields and how objects attract and repel each other. They will develop their communication skills through discussing their observations.

Taking it forward
- Give the children a range of different sized magnets and ask them to make predictions about which ones will have the strongest magnetic fields and why.

Top tip
This activity works best with a magnetic wand, though any large magnet that is easy to hold is fine.

Health & Safety
Supervise young children carefully with paperclips and make sure they don't put them in their mouths.

Scan the QR code to see a video of this activity.

Electromagnets
Understanding magnetic force

What you need:
- Magnetic wands or large magnets (one per child)
- Batteries (one per child)
- Small metal objects (paper clips, bells, pennies, and so on)

What to do:
1. Gather the children. Revisit what they already know about magnets and explain that they will be learning about electromagnets today.
2. Give each child a battery and ask them if the battery can pick up a paper clip.
3. Show the children what happens when you attach a magnetic wand to the battery, then ask the children how many paper clips they could attach.
4. Explain to the children that the magnetic force goes through the battery, making it an electromagnet, so it's able to pick up small metal objects.

What's in it for the children?
The children develop their learning about magnetic forces, attraction and repulsion. They also develop their numeracy skills through counting how many paperclips will attract to the battery.

Taking it forward
- Develop children's counting skills by getting them to count how many objects can attach to the electromagnet at once. Introduce simple tally or bar charts as a way of recording the information.
- Experiment with different types of batteries and paperclips, or use multiple magnetic wands. For each different variation, ask the children to predict what might happen and explain their thinking.

Health & Safety
Supervise young children carefully to make sure that they do not put any small objects into their mouths.

Top tip
If using uncoated paper clips (the ordinary silver ones) the effect of the magnetic force in the battery lingers for a longer time. This means that when you remove the magnetic wand, the paper clips will still stick to the battery.

Lifting a jar of rice with a pencil
Learning about friction

What you need:
- Jars or empty spice bottles (one per child)
- Pencils (one per child)
- Measuring jugs
- Uncooked rice

What to do:
1. Gather the children and ask them if they think they can pick up a jar full of rice with a pencil. Discuss their answers, then ask if they know what friction means.
2. Explain to them that friction is when two items (or in the case of this activity the grains of rice) are packed so tightly around the pencil, it prevents any movement.
3. Give each child a small jar or empty spice bottle and a pencil.
4. Give the children the measuring jugs and ask them to measure out the rice to fill the jars.
5. Show them how to gently push the rice in with their fingers so that it compacts around the pencil.
6. Ask the children to try lifting the pencil at regular intervals to check if the rice has interlocked or compacted around the pencil. When it does, the child will be able to lift the jar of rice with the pencil.

What's in it for the children?
The children learn new vocabulary: friction, compact and interlocking. They also develop their maths learning by using a measuring jug to measure how much rice to go in the jar.

Taking it forward
- Encourage the children to explore other materials to put in the jars (for example dried beans, small toys and so on) to see if the effect is the same.
- Ask the children to predict which material they think would be most effective.

Top tip
Ask the children to bring in empty jars from home to encourage sustainability.

 Scan the QR code to see a video of this activity.

Finding the centre of gravity

Learning about gravity and balance

What you need:
- Craft sticks (one per child)
- Pipe cleaners (one per child)
- Clothes pegs (two per child)

What's in it for the children?
The children gain an understanding of what gravity is and how to find the centre of gravity. They will also develop their fine motor and concentration skills.

Taking it forward
- Ask the children to try balancing different equipment like pencils or rulers and ask them to discuss what they have seen.

What to do:

1. Gather the children and explain that they will doing an activity on finding the centre of gravity.
2. Ask the children what they know about gravity. Discuss their answers and then explain to them that gravity is the force that pulls everything towards the centre of the Earth. (For more about this see Layers of the Earth p. 20.)
3. Give each child a craft stick, pipe cleaner and two clothes pegs.
4. Pick up the craft stick and try and hold it upright so that it balances on your finger. Ask the children what they could do to help keep the craft stick upright.
5. Take the pipe cleaner and wrap it around once at the bottom of the craft stick, so that the two ends of the pipe cleaner hang downwards.
6. Attach one clothes peg to one end of the pipe cleaner. Then attach the other clothes peg to the other end of the pipe cleaner. The craft stick should balance upright. This is the centre of gravity.
7. Let the children have a go for themselves, encouraging them to ask questions and discuss their observations.

Top tip
All of these resources are available cheaply online or from a craft shop.

Creating craters
Exploring gravity

What you need:
- Pictures or videos of craters on the moon
- Trays
- Flour or sand
- Different sized marbles, balls and pom poms
- Paint

What's in it for the children?
The children learn about gravity, impact and the craters that are created when something heavy falls into something soft. They are also learning how to make and test predictions when trying out dropping different objects.

Taking it forward
- Ask the children to drop paint-soaked pom poms into water and ask them to discuss what they see.
- Ask them to drop them on paper and compare the differences and similarities between the impact of a pom pom on water, paper and flour.

Health & Safety
Carefully supervise young children with marbles.

What to do:
1. Ask the children what they know about gravity. Show them pictures or videos of craters on the moon.
2. Spread the flour out evenly onto trays so that each tray has the same thick layer.
3. Ask the children what they think might happen if marbles are dropped from a height onto flour.
4. Ask each child to drop different sized marbles onto the flour from different heights, ask them to discuss their observations. They will find that the indents will be of different sizes depending on the height the marbles were dropped from.
5. Give each child some different sized pom poms that have been soaked in paint and ask them to drop them into the tray of flour. Ask them if they can see the difference between dropping marbles and pom poms.
6. Give them dry pom poms and ask them to record their observations.
7. Ask them if soaking the pom poms in paint made any difference. Discuss weight and what happens when something heavy falls onto something soft.

Newton's tumbling beads
Exploring a famous experiment

What you need:
- Strings of plastic beads
- Glasses or jars

What to do:
1. Gather the children and explain that today they will be learning about Issac Newton who was a scientist in the 1600s. He came up with his theory of gravity after an apple fell on his head.
2. Show the children the strings of beads and ask them to carefully put them into their jar or glass.
3. Pull one end of the bead string out so that it dangles just over the mouth of the jar.
4. Lift the jar up high and ask the children to observe what happens.
5. Gently tug the end and let go. The beads will tumble out automatically on their own.
6. Let the children have a turn and ask them why they think the beads might be falling out on their own.
7. Discuss their answers and then explain that gravity pulls the string of beads to the ground.

Health & Safety
Remind the children not to put the beads into their mouth or around their necks.

What's in it for the children?
The children learn about Isaac Newton and one of his famous experiments. They get to apply what they already know about gravity to new learning and see it in action.

Taking it forward
- Try the same activity using different weights of bead strings and ask the children to predict what they think might happen first.

 Scan the QR code to see a video of this activity.

Top tip
You can buy the beads cheaply online or from your local pound shop.

The shape of water

Learning that water has no shape

What you need:

- Jugs
- Water
- Transparent containers (varying sizes)
- Food colouring

What to do:

1. Gather the children and ask them what shape they think water is. Then ask them to pour water from the jug into different container shapes. Let them squeeze a few drops of different food colouring into the containers.
2. As the children are pouring water into the containers, ask them to look carefully at the water flowing from the jug.
3. Explain to the children that water has no shape and that it takes the shape of whatever container it is poured into.
4. Ask the children to look around them to see what other shapes water can change into.

What's in it for the children?

Through this activity the children learn that water is free-flowing and takes the shape of the container it is poured into.

Taking it forward

- Introduce new vocabulary: solids, liquids, freezing and melting.
- Freeze some of the water into ice cubes and then leave them in the Sun to demonstrate how some solids can melt easily to become liquids.

Top tip

Add different food colouring to each container of water to make the activity more visually appealing.

Electrolysis
Splitting water into hydrogen and oxygen

What you need:
- Cardboard
- Scissors
- Pencil sharpener
- Pencils (two per group)
- Water
- Glasses (one per group)
- Alligator clip cables (two per group)
- 9V batteries (one per group)

What to do:
1. Gather the children and explain to them that water is made of hydrogen and oxygen.
2. Ask them if they think it is possible to split the water up into hydrogen and oxygen. Explain that it is possible by using the electric current from a 9V battery.
3. Cut a piece of cardboard into a square and sharpen both ends of two pencils.
4. Ask the children to carefully pour the water into a glass, then ask them to place the cardboard square on top.
5. Poke the two pencils through the cardboard, then attach one end of each of the alligator clips to the pencil leads and the other end to the connectors on the V9 battery.
6. Ask the children to look at the pencils that are in the water.
7. The pencil lead with the most bubbles indicates the presence of hydrogen. The other pencil lead with less bubbles indicates the presence of oxygen. This is because there are two atoms of hydrogen and only one atom of oxygen.

Top tip
This activity is most effective in small groups so that the children can see the bubbles clearly.

30

50 fantastic ideas for STEM

What's in it for the children?

The children learn that water is made of hydrogen and oxygen and can discuss the changes that are happening in front of them as they take place.

Taking it forward

- Add two teaspoons of salt to the water to see if there is any change to the bubbles.
- Ask the children to predict what might happen first and discuss their observations.

Travelling water
How water sticks

What you need:
- Glasses
- String (wool based)
- Scissors
- Gaffer tape
- Water
- Food colouring (optional)
- Trays (optional)

What to do:
1. Gather the children and ask them what they know about water.
2. Explain that water molecules are made up of hydrogen and oxygen (see Electrolysis p. 30) and that water molecules like to hug other water molecules.
3. Put a glass on the table, then cut a piece of string about 30 cm long.
4. Stick one end of the string onto the inside of the glass using the gaffer tape.
5. Pour some water into the glass and let the string soak. Squeeze a drop of food colouring into the water so that it is easier to see.
6. Pull the string out of the water, ensuring that the bottom end is still attached to the bottom of the glass.
7. Gently lift the glass up and pour the water down the string into a second glass or tray on the table.
8. The water will follow the string because the string is wet and water molecules is adhesive and sticks to other water molecules.

What's in it for the children?
This activity teaches children that water is adhesive or sticky due to hydrogen bonds, which enable water molecules to stick to a wet string.

Taking it forward
- Ask the children what might happen if you tried to pour water down a dry length of string (without soaking it first).
- Be prepared for them to make a mess while testing out their predictions!

Top tip
Use string made of wool to get the desired effect. This activity is best done outside but use a tray if inside as it can get messy!

Scan the QR code to see a video of this activity.

Floating water
Learning about vacuum seals

What you need:
- Glasses (one per child)
- Water
- Food colouring
- Scissors
- Cardboard (thick)
- Trays
- Paper towels

What to do:
1. Gather the children and explain to them that you are going to make water float in an upside-down glass.
2. Fill a glass halfway with water and squirt in a few drops of food colouring.
3. Cut a square of cardboard and put it over the glass.
4. Press down firmly with the palm of your hand and turn the glass upside down.
5. Slowly remove your hand from the cardboard. The water in the glass will appear to be floating.
6. Explain to the children that pressing your palm on the cardboard creates a vacuum seal around the glass, keeping the liquid in. However, if bubbles appear while pressing down it means that air is escaping and the seal is not secure.
7. Let each child have a turn at making water float. Make sure to have plenty of paper towels and a tray in case of any spillages.

Top tip
A smooth piece of cardboard will create a good seal. It needs to be dry, not damp.

What's in it for the children?
This activity shows children how a vacuum seal can be created with a glass half-full of water. The children will be amazed by science in action and will want to ask lots of questions, developing their communication skills.

Taking it forward
- Let the children experiment with different liquids such as soapy water, oil or vinegar, and ask the children to predict what they think might happen with each one.

 Scan the QR code to see a video of this activity.

Sticks through bags of water

Providing co-regulatory buddies

What you need:

- Sealable food bags (one per child)
- Food colouring
- Water
- Wooden skewers or sharp pencils (five or six per child)
- Trays
- Paper towels

What to do:

1. Gather the children and ask them what they think will happen if they poke a skewer through a bag of water.
2. Squirt a few drops of food colouring into each bag and fill the bags with water. Seal each bag when it is almost full.
3. Give the bags to the children (hold it for them if they are younger than three) then ask them to poke a skewer right through the bag.
4. The water stays in the bag and doesn't leak out. Ask the children if they know why this happens.
5. Explain to them that a plastic seal is created around the entry and exit points of the skewer making it watertight. However, if the pencils or skewers are pulled out, the water will pour out of the holes.

What's in it for the children?

This fun and exciting activity will help the children to understand that plastic can stretch and contract, creating a seal around a skewer.

Taking it forward

- Let the children experiment with different liquids such as oil or sparkling water.
- Encourage the children's measuring skills by getting them to measure their own liquids before putting them in the bags.

Health & Safety

Supervise the children carefully when they are pushing the skewers through the bags.

Top tip

Use trays and keep lots of paper towels ready – this activity can get messy!

Rescuing toys trapped in ice
Exploring freezing and melting

What you need:
- Small toys (people or animals)
- Large ice tray (or plastic container)
- Two bowls
- Water (warm and cold)
- Pipettes
- Salt

What's in it for the children?
The children will build on their learning about melting and freezing and will be able to discuss the changes they see happening. Using pipettes will help to improve their fine motor skills.

Taking it forward
- Combine this activity with small world play or a superhero topic to spark the children's imaginations!

What to do:
1. Freeze some small toys in a large tray or container.
2. Gather the children and explain to them that there are toys trapped in the ice. Ask them how they might be able to rescue them.
3. Let the children touch the ice and describe what they feel. Revisit what the children might already know about melting and freezing (see Painting on ice p.19).
4. Put down two bowls of water, one warm and the other cool.
5. Give each child a pipette and ask them to suck up the cool water first and squirt it over the ice. Ask them to discuss what they have seen.
6. Repeat using the warm water.
7. Give them a small bowl of salt and ask them what they think might happen if they sprinkle it on the ice. Let them investigate.
8. Ask the children to feel the texture of the ice when it's covered with salt and ask them to observe what happens.
9. Let them continue squirting water over the ice until the toys are released.
10. Once the toys are released from the ice, ask the children what they think worked the best and why.

Lava lamp
Learning that oil and water do not mix

What you need:
- Pictures or videos of lava lamps
- Measuring jugs
- Large glasses or vases (one per lava lamp)
- Water (400 ml per lava lamp)
- Vegetable oil (800 ml per lava lamp)
- Food colouring
- Fizzing tablets

What to do:
1. Gather the children and show them pictures or videos of lava lamps. Explain that they will be making their own versions in pairs or small groups.
2. Ask one of the children to pour the water into a large glass or vase using a measuring jug and ask another child to pour some oil into the large glass or vase.
3. Ask the children to choose one food colouring bottle each and squirt one drop into the oil. Ask the children to observe what happens.
4. Explain to the children that the molecules of oil are 'hydrophobic' and do not like to mix with the molecules of water, so they stay on the top of the water. However, the drops of food colouring get heavy and then drop into the water.
5. Give each child a fizzing tablet and ask them to drop it into the large glass or vase.
6. Ask the children to observe what happens to the oil, water and food colouring.
7. Explain to the children that the fizzing tablet reacts with the water and creates a carbon dioxide gas, which are the bubbles that the children can see.
8. The bubbles attach to the food colouring, travel upwards and then pop, releasing the food colouring back through the oil and into the water, creating a lava lamp effect.

What's in it for the children?

The children will develop their measuring skills and use their communication skills as they observe what is happening. They will also learn, in a colourful and immersive way, that oil and water do not mix.

Taking it forward

- Use a spoonful of bicarb instead of fizzing tablets and bells instead of food colouring.
- Ask the children to discuss their observations and predictions.

Top tip

Use only one colour per lava lamp as too many will spoil the effect.

50 fantastic ideas for STEM

Buoyancy
Learning about floating and sinking

What you need:
- Water
- Glasses (one per child or group)
- Oranges (one per child or group)

What to do:
1. Gather the children and introduce the new vocabulary: floating, sinking and buoyancy. Relate it to things they know – for example, bath toys or boats.
2. Discuss what they think would happen if they put an orange in water.
3. Give each child (or group) a full glass of water.
4. Give half of the children a peeled orange and the other half an unpeeled orange.
5. Count down from three and at one tell the children to drop their oranges into the glasses of water.
6. Ask the children what they have observed and ask them why they think one orange sank and one didn't.
7. Explain to the children that the unpeeled orange is protected by the orange peel which is full of air bubbles and so helps the orange to stay afloat. Let the children feel the orange peel so they can see it for themselves.

What's in it for the children?
The children learn new vocabulary and can relate it to their prior knowledge about floating and sinking. They can communicate their ideas, ask questions and make predictions.

Taking it forward
- Extend the activity to testing out different fruits and vegetables to see which ones float and why.
- Link the activity with small world play and make a boating lake – give the children a range of toy boats and let them compare which ones float best and why.

Sneezing noses

Learning about how germs spread

What you need:
- Balloons (pre-cut, one per child or group)
- Empty kitchen roll tubes (quartered, one per child or group)
- Pom poms
- Tissues

What to do:
1. Gather the children and ask them what happens when they sneeze. Ask them what they know about germs and how they spread.
2. Explain that they are going to make a sneezing nose and learn how germs are spread when someone sneezes without covering their mouth and nose with a tissue.
3. Give each child or group one balloon, with the neck already cut off, and one quarter of kitchen roll tube.
4. Ask the children to help each other pull part of their balloon over the end of a quarter of kitchen roll tube.
5. Ask the children to loosely fill the tubes with pom poms.
6. Ask the children to pull the balloon at the back of the tube (like a catapult) to force the pom poms out. Explain to them that when someone sneezes the germs fly all over the place just like the pom poms.
7. Ask the children to repeat the activity using a tissue to catch the pom poms. There will be some pom poms that still manage to escape despite the tissue.

What's in it for the children?
This fun and visual activity helps the children learn about how germs spread and link it to their prior knowledge on why they should catch germs with a tissue.

Taking it forward
- Develop the children's counting skills by asking them to count the number of germs that are sneezed out of the noses.
- Ask the children to make handprints in flour and then touch black paper. This is another visual activity to show children how germs are spread and the importance of washing their hands.

Top tip ⭐
Ask the children to bring in empty kitchen roll tubes from home to encourage recycling. Pre-cut the kitchen roll tubes into quarters and the necks off the balloons before starting the activity.

 Scan the QR code to see a video of this activity.

Pumping lungs
Learning how we breathe

What you need:
- Elastic bands (two per group)
- Large balloons (three per group)
- Bendy straws (two per group)
- A large plastic bottle (cut in half)
- Scissors
- Sticky tack

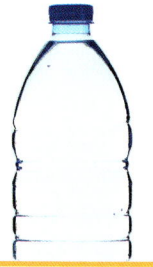

What to do:
1. Gather the children and ask them what they know about our lungs and how we breathe. Let the children look at picture books about lungs in the body. Show them how lungs work and how we breathe in and out.
2. Explain to the children that their diaphragm is a thin dome-shaped muscle below their lungs and helps with breathing. Ask them to take a deep breath in and release.
3. Use the elastic band to attach one balloon to the end of the straw. Do the same with the other straw.
4. Push both straws through the top of the bottle, leaving only the bendy parts of the straw sticking out.
5. Seal the top of the bottle with sticky tack to make an airtight seal. Then cut the neck off the remaining balloon and stretch it over the bottom of the bottle. This is the diaphragm.
6. Show the children how when the diaphragm is gently pulled, the balloons (lungs) in the bottle (the rib cage), inflate with air, when the diaphragm is pushed upwards the balloons (lungs) deflate.
7. Show them how the pushing and pulling of the balloon inflates and delates the balloons on the straws, just like the lungs in the human body.

Top tip
Cut the bottles in half and smooth out any rough edges before starting the activity. This activity is best done in pairs or small groups.

What's in it for the children?

The children learn how their lungs work and can discuss what they see as it happens. They can link this knowledge to what they already know about the human body and discuss why our lungs are important.

Taking it forward

- Use this activity as part of a topic on the human body: get the children to work in pairs and ask one child to lie down on a large piece of paper while the other draws an outline around them. Stick the lungs onto the body and use as a wall display which can be added to when learning about different body parts.

Health & Safety
Supervise the children carefully when using elastic bands.

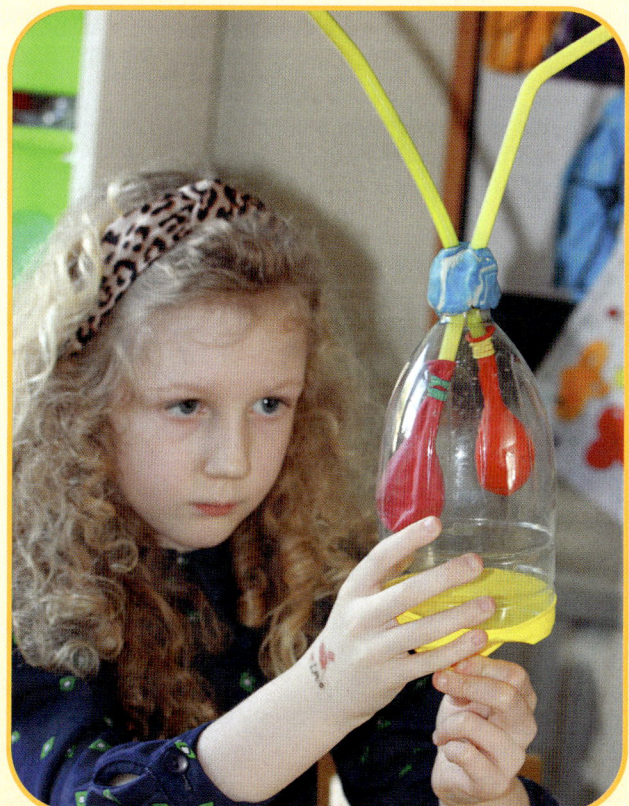

Exploring sound
Visible vibrations

What you need:
- Musical instruments (optional)
- A portable music speaker
- Cling film
- Sand, rice or salt

What to do:
1. Gather the children and ask them what they know about sound and how we hear it. Talk about the musical instruments that the children know, let them explore some if available.
2. Explain to them that their ears help them to hear sound and sound can also be seen and felt through vibrations.
3. Put the portable speaker, covered in cling film, face up on the table.
4. Ask the children to put some sand, rice or salt onto the speaker.
5. Turn the speaker on and ask the children to observe what happens.

What's in it for the children?
The children learn about how we hear sounds because of the vibrations that they make. They will be able to link this to their prior knowledge about musical instruments.

Taking it forward
- Cover a bowl with cling film and pour some salt or rice on the top, or fill a bowl with water and ask the children to shout hello at it. Get them to discuss what they see.
- Introduce the idea of sound volume: what would happen to the vibrations if the children whispered instead of shouted?

Scan the QR code to see a video of this activity.

Top tip
Wrap the speaker up with cling film before the start of the activity to protect it.

Layers of the skin
Exploring the composition of skin

What you need:
- White and red pom poms
- Red play dough
- Pipe cleaners
- Scissors

What to do:
1. Gather the children and ask them what they know about skin.
2. Explain that the skin is the largest organ in the human body, and it has three layers. The first layer is called the epidermis, which protects the body and it is the layer through which hair grows. The second layer is the dermis, which also contains the sweat glands. The last layer is called the hypodermis, which stores the cells of fat. Discuss with the children why they think each layer is important.
3. Ask the children to lay out the white pom poms and explain that it's the hypodermis.
4. Ask them to put the red pom poms on top which is the dermis.
5. Finally ask them to roll out the red play dough and put it over red pom poms, this layer is the hypodermis.
6. Cut the pipe cleaners into small pieces and ask the children to stick the pieces into the play dough to represent the hair on the skin.

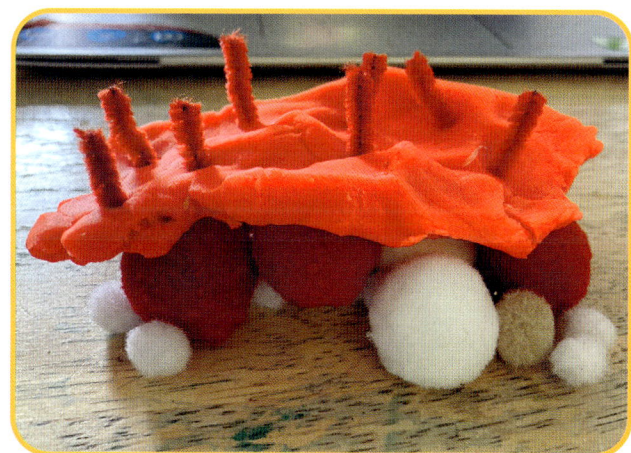

What's in it for the children?
The children learn new vocabulary: epidermis, dermis and hypodermis. They can relate what they have learnt to their everyday lives, such as when they fall and graze their knees. Manipulating play dough helps to develop their fine motor skills.

Taking it forward
- Use this activity as part of a topic on the human body.
- Get the children to make pictures of the layers of the skin to add to a wall display on different body parts (see Pumping lungs p. 40).

Top tip
All of these materials are available cheaply online from any craft shop. Alternatives are balls of tissue paper instead of pom poms and red card instead of play dough.

Pumping hearts

Learning how the heart pumps blood

What you need:

- Jars
- Water
- Red food colouring
- Scissors
- Balloons (one per child or group)
- Bendy straws (two per child or group)
- Sticky tape

What to do:

1. Gather the children around the table and ask them what they know about how blood pumps round the body. Explain to them that they will be making their own heart mechanisms.

2. Ask the children to fill the jars with water to the top, then ask them to squirt a few drops of red food colouring in. This represents the blood.

3. Cut the neck off the balloon and stretch it over a jar. Then gently poke two holes into the stretched balloon and push the straws into the holes with the bendy parts sticking out.

4. Put the cut off balloon neck over one of the bendy parts and keep it in place with sticky tape. Loosely seal the top with sticky tape.

5. Gently push the balloon downwards using a pumping action, this will release the blood through the straw.

6. Explain to the children that the loosely sealed straw is a heart valve. There are four valves in the heart and they open and close to let the blood flow from one area to another. The opening and closing of the valves make the sound of the heartbeat. The straw through which the blood pumps out is the artery.

50 fantastic ideas for STEM

What's in it for the children?

The children gain an understanding of how the heart pumps blood. They will improve their communication skills as they discuss what they can see happening.

Taking it forward

- Link this activity to a topic about healthy living and exercise by getting the children to feel their pulses before and after running.

- Get the children to draw pictures of their hearts to add to a human body wall display (see Pumping lungs p. 40).

Top tip

Have the children look at picture books that describe the working of the heart and how it pumps blood all around the body.

Composition of blood
Learning what blood is made of

What you need:
- A large tray
- Red pom poms (small)
- White pom poms (medium)
- Pink felt
- Scissors
- Plastic test tubes (one per child)
- Funnels

What to do:
1. Put the tray of red and white pom poms in the middle of the table. The red pom poms are the red blood cells and the white pom poms are the white blood cells. There should be more red pom poms than white ones.
2. Cut the felt into small rectangles and scatter them over the red pom poms. These are the platelets.
3. Gather the children and ask them what they already know about blood. Explain to them that their blood is made of red blood cells, white blood cells, platelets and plasma.
4. Ask the children what they think the white blood cells and platelets do. Explain that the white blood cells fight infection when they are unwell, and platelets are their bodies' natural plasters when they get hurt.
5. Explain to them that the plasma is the liquid part of blood in their bodies and helps the blood to flow.
6. Ask the children to put the pom poms into test tubes using the funnel. Explain to them that the test tubes represent the arteries and veins in the body through which the blood flows.

What's in it for the children?
The children are introduced to new vocabulary and learn what makes up the blood in their bodies.

Taking it forward
- Ask the children to make a large figure out of play dough or clay and push the test tubes into the arms and legs to demonstrate blood in the body.

46

50 fantastic ideas for STEM

Making a working well
Understanding simple pulley systems

What you need:
- Juice or milk cartons (1 litre, with lid)
- Scissors
- Jugs
- Water
- Food colouring
- Pencils or wooden skewers (one per well)
- String
- Bulldog clips (one per well)

What to do:
1. Gather the children and discuss wells with them. Ask them if they have seen a well and where they might find one.
2. Ask them what they think might help to draw water out of the well. Discuss pulley systems and how they work.
3. Cut a large square window out of the top half of the carton.
4. Fill the jugs with water. Ask the children to squirt some food colouring into them.
5. Ask the children to pour the water into the bottom half of the carton.
6. Stick a pencil or skewer through the top half of the carton, so that the ends stick out on either side.
7. Cut the string 10 cm long. Tie one end to the middle of the pencil and the other end to the handle of the bulldog clip, then attach the bulldog clip to the lid of the carton. This is the bucket.
8. Let the bucket fall into the water. Ask the children to carefully wind one end of the pencil to pull up the bucket with some water. The children have now made a working well using a simple pulley system.

What's in it for the children?
The children learn about push and pull forces and develop their fine motor skills when making their wells.

Taking it forward
- Use your working wells as part of small world play, using small toy people and animals to spark the children's imagination.

Top tip ★
Add blue food colouring to the water so it can be clearly seen.

Making a working catapult
Get ready for lift off!

What you need:
- Craft sticks (four per catapult)
- Elastic bands (three per catapult)
- Pom poms
- Plastic spoons (optional)

What's in it for the children?
This fun and exciting activity helps the children to understand the mechanisms of a catapult. Making the catapults will help to develop the children's fine motor skills and working together, encourages a sense of team work and improves social skills.

Taking it forward
- Develop the children's measuring skills by comparing how far two pom poms can fly and measuring the distance between them.
- Create a basketball hoop with pipe cleaners and ask the children to shoot pom poms through the hoop.

Health & Safety
Supervise the children carefully when using elastic bands.

What to do:
1. Gather the children and discuss what catapults are and what they were used for in the past. Talk about what forces are being used and discuss what the children think pulling and pushing mean.
2. Explain that the children will be making their own working catapults.
3. Stack two craft sticks, then wrap an elastic band on either end.
4. Stack the other two craft sticks and wrap the remaining elastic band at one end to create a V shape.
5. Slip this V shape over the stacked craft sticks to create a cross shape. Gently tap one arm of the V downwards. It should ping back.
6. Place the pom pom on the arm of the V and press it down and let go. It should catapult off.
7. Optional: attach a plastic spoon to the arm of the V and use the spoon to catapult the pom pom by pressing it downwards.

Scan the QR code to see a video of this activity.

Building with paper
Testing the strength of paper

What you need:
- Paper
- Magazines or catalogues
- Sticky tape
- Board books

What to do:
1. Gather the children and ask them if paper could hold up a heavy book. Give them a range of paper and magazines and some time to investigate on their own. Ask them which ones might work best and how to make them stronger.
2. Ask the children to work together to roll up the paper or magazines and secure them with sticky tape.
3. Stand four columns of rolled paper in a square and ask a child to place a board book on top. Ask the children what they think might happen.
4. Repeat this until you have a tall tower! Give the children the chance to do this in pairs or groups and encourage them to think about the best ways to stop their towers from toppling.

Top tip
This is a great activity to encourage teamwork and develop the children's communication skills.

What's in it for the children?
The children use trial and error and have a go at finding different ways to reach their goal. They learn communication and social skills through working together.

Taking it forward
- Encourage the children to predict other materials that might be stronger than paper and give them a chance to try out building towers with them.
- Encourage imaginative small world play by asking the children to build a town or city. Add in toys and give the children a chance to discuss what buildings they would need.

Making a conveyor belt
Engineering and movement

What you need:
- Rectangular tissue boxes (empty, one per child)
- Scissors
- Pencils (two per child)
- Elastic bands (four per child)
- Kitchen roll
- Sticky tape

What to do:
1. Gather the children and ask them if they know what a conveyor belt is and where they might have seen one before (for example, at a supermarket or airport). Explain that they will be making a conveyor belt out of a tissue box.
2. Make four holes at either end of the long side of the tissue box.
3. Take two pencils and wrap an elastic band around each end. Keep the elastic bands toward the middle of the pencils, about 6 cm apart.
4. Push the pencils with the elastic bands through the holes in the tissue box.
5. Cut a square of kitchen roll in half and attach the short ends to create one long strip.
6. Feed this strip over the elastic bands in the box. Cut off the excess kitchen roll and tape the ends together.
7. Take the ends of the two pencils closest to you and twirl them in the same direction to rotate the kitchen roll. It should rotate smoothly, like a conveyor belt.

Top tip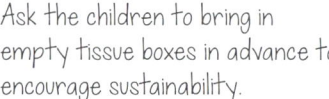
Ask the children to bring in empty tissue boxes in advance to encourage sustainability.

What's in it for the children?

The children learn the mechanism of a basic conveyor belt and can relate it to their prior knowledge.

Taking it forward

- Use the conveyor belts as part of small world play: get the children to draw pictures of supermarket items, cut them out and use them on their conveyor belts.

✚ Health & Safety
Supervise the children carefully when using elastic bands.

Scan the QR code to see a video of this activity.

50 fantastic ideas for STEM

Making a maze
A fun way to learn directions

What you need:
- Trays, foil or a table cover
- Play dough
- Pom poms (medium)
- Straws

What to do:
1. Gather the children and ask them if they have been to a maze before and what it might mean if not.
2. Explain that you will be showing them how to create a maze from play dough.
3. Help them to roll out the play dough into strips and then create a maze with an entry and exit point.
4. Introduce positional language: left, right, straight, forwards, backwards.
5. Give the children the pom poms and ask them to use the straws to blow the pom poms from the entry point to the exit point. If working in pairs, the children could take turns with one child blowing the pom pom and the other telling them the direction to blow it in.

What's in it for the children?
The children learn positional vocabulary and develop their communication skills. Manipulating play dough helps to develop their hand strength and fine motor skills.

Taking it forward
- Test different materials for making mazes (cardboard, paper, LEGO® and so on.) Get the children to predict which will be the most effective.

Top tip
Use a large tray to make your maze in or cover the table with foil or a cover before you start.

 Scan the QR code to see a video of this activity.

52

50 fantastic ideas for STEM

Sundial
Learning about light, shadows and time

What you need:
- Pictures or videos of sun dials (optional)
- Paper plates (one per child)
- Pencils (one per child)
- Sunlight
- Clocks (toy or real)

What to do:
1. Gather the children and ask them if they know what a sundial might be or if they have seen one before. Relate their answers to what they already know about time.
2. Explain to them that a sundial is an outdoor clock that uses the sun to tell the time. Ask them how they think this happens and relate it to what they already know about shadows.
3. Demonstrate by drawing the clock face with all the numbers on the back of a paper plate.
4. Stick a pencil through the plate and put it in the sun. Put a wall clock alongside.
5. Ask the children to observe where the pencil's shadow falls and then ask them if it matches with the time shown on the wall clock.
6. Help the children make their own sundials.

What's in it for the children?
The children learn about light and how shadows are created. They can relate it to their daily routines and what they know already about time. They can build on their mathematical learning by understanding what the numbers on a clock mean.

Taking it forward
- Get the children to make their own clocks: create a small hand and big hand from cardboard and use a split pin attach them to the centre of a paper plate.
- Make it relevant to their daily routines. For example, twelve o' clock is lunch time.

Top tip
This activity works best outdoors on a sunny day. Use it as part of a topic on shadows, time or daily routines.

Painting coloured shadows
Exploring light and colour

What you need:
- Coloured cellophane (pre-cut into squares)
- White paper
- Torches (one per child)
- Paintbrushes
- Paint

What's in it for the children?
The children build on their prior knowledge of light and shadows and are introduced to new vocabulary on the topic. They will be able to explore colour and colour mixing and develop their expressive art and design skills.

Taking it forward
- Create stained glass windows: cut window shapes out of card, then ask the children to stick coloured cellophane pieces in. This would look lovely as a wall display.
- Look at different materials that make coloured shadows (magnetic tiles, for example) and paint pictures using those.

What to do:
1. Gather the children and ask them what they know about light and shadows. Introduce and discuss new vocabulary: transparent, translucent and opaque.
2. Demonstrate how to position the coloured cellophane in front of the white paper and place the torch behind it. Ask the children to discuss what they see.
3. Give the children the torches and cellophane and let them explore.
4. Give each child a piece of white paper and access to the paints and paintbrushes.
5. Ask the children to paint the coloured shadows using the same colours, for example blue shadows should be painted blue and so forth. However, if the children want to change colours and have fun mixing colours, then let them.

Top tip
Pre-cut the cellophane into manageable squares before the activity starts.

Colouring water with light
Investigating transparency

What you need:
- Glasses of different sizes
- Water
- Torches
- Coloured cellophane (pre-cut into squares)
- Coloured plastic (magnetic tiles, for example)
- Elastic bands

What to do:
1. Gather the children and show them the glasses of water. Ask them what they could do to change the colour of the water and discuss their answers.
2. Give each child a torch (or ask them to share) and a piece of coloured cellophane or coloured plastic.
3. Wrap the cellophane around the torch and secure it with an elastic band, turn the torch on and shine it over the water in the glass. Alternatively, place a piece of coloured plastic over the glass and ask the children to shine the light through it.
4. Ask the children to observe the colour of the water.
5. Let them play with different coloured cellophane or plastic to see which combinations of light and glass shape make stronger colours in the water.

What's in it for the children?
The children build on their learning about colour, shadow and light and develop their communication skills as they observe the changes the light makes to the water.

Taking it forward
- Get the children to create a light show set to music and record it using a tablet or video camera.

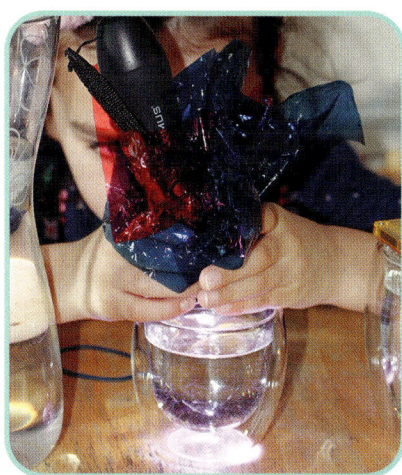

Health & Safety
Carefully supervise the children when using elastic bands.

50 fantastic ideas for STEM

Capillary rainbows
Growing rainbows using capillary action

What you need:
- Kitchen roll
- Kitchen roll adverts (pictures or video)
- Non-permanent marker pens (rainbow colours)
- Water
- A jug
- A tray

What to do:
1. Gather the children. Ask them to discuss what they know about kitchen roll and what we use it for. Introduce new vocabulary: absorbency and capillary action (when the water is sucked up through the paper). Show the children adverts of different kitchen roll brands, which say how absorbent they are.
2. Give the children some sheets of kitchen roll and ask them to draw thick vertical lines at the bottom, keeping the lines close together.
3. Ask them to pour water from the jug into the tray.
4. Then ask them to hold the coloured end of the kitchen roll in the water and count to ten.
5. Ask the children to watch their lines grow as the water is pulled through the kitchen roll. Discuss their observations.
6. While the children watch their rainbows grow, ask them what they think is happening and why.

What's in it for the children?
The children learn about capillary action and can discuss the changes that they see happening in front of them. This activity also encourages the children to develop their fine motor as well as expressive art and design skills.

Taking it forward
- Put some food colouring in a vase of flowers and ask the children to observe what happens. The best flowers to use are white flowers like roses, dahlias and gerberas.
- Test out different brands of kitchen roll to see which one has the best capillary action by investigating which rainbow grows the fastest.

Making rainbows outside
Learning about light refraction

What you need:
- A hose
- Outside area

What's in it for the children?
The children get to explore their outside surroundings while learning about light refraction. They can build on their prior knowledge of light and rainbows and develop their communication skills while discussing their ideas.

Taking it forward
- Show the children other examples of light refraction: create a rainbow by shining a torch on the silver side of a CD.

What to do:
1. Gather the children and ask them to discuss what they already know about rainbows.
2. Explain to them that a rainbow is formed when the white sunlight (which is a combination of all visible colours) falls on raindrops. The light bends (refracts) and splits into the seven different colours that we can see.
3. Take the children outside into the garden or open area.
4. Turn on the hose and spray it, making sure that the sunlight is falling over the spray. A rainbow should appear; change position if necessary.
5. Ask the children to discuss which colours they can see.
6. Let the children take turns using the hose to create their own rainbows.

Top tip
This works best on a bright and sunny day. Prepare to get wet!

Outlining shadows
Learning how shadows are made

What you need:
- White paper
- Pencils (black)
- Small wooden toys or LEGO® figures
- Torches (one per child)

What to do:
1. Give each child a piece of paper, a black pencil and a torch. Discuss what they know already about shadows (see Sundial p. 53).
2. Ask them to choose some toys they like and stand them upright along top edge of the paper.
3. Show them how to carefully outline the shadow on their paper.
4. Demonstrate how the shadow can grow, shrink or move to the opposite side just by changing the position and direction of the torch. Let them experiment.

What's in it for the children?
The children build on their prior knowledge of shadows and use their communication skills to discuss their ideas. Drawing the outlines of objects helps to strengthen their hand muscles, and improves their fine motor skills and pencil control.

Taking it forward
- Link this activity with repeating patterns by asking the children to create their own repeating pattern shadow outline.
- Take the activity outside and get the children to take turns drawing each other's shadows in chalk.

Light refraction with three glasses
Colour mixing from different angles

What you need:
- Transparent glasses or jars (three per group)
- A tray
- Water
- A jug
- Food colouring (red, yellow and blue)

What to do:
1. Gather the children and explain that they will be doing an activity on light refraction. Explain that light travels in a straight line and bends when it goes through different substances, changing our perception (how we see things).
2. Place three glasses on a tray and ask the children to fill them almost to the top with water using the jug.
3. Then ask them to squirt in two drops of red food colouring in one glass, yellow in the other and then blue.
4. Position the glass with yellow food colouring in the front of the glasses with blue and red food colouring.
5. Ask the children to look through the yellow glass towards the blue glass from the side and ask them what they can see. They should see green.
6. Ask them to look through the yellow towards the red and they should see orange.
7. Ask them to look through the red to the blue and they should see purple.
8. Explain to the children that light bends or curves as it travels through the glasses, giving the illusion of a different colour.

Top tip
This activity works well on a sunny day.

What's in it for the children?
The children build on their knowledge of light refraction and that it means bending of light. They also explore colour mixing.

Taking it forward
- A very simple but effective light refraction activity is putting a pencil into a glass half-full of water so that it looks bendy. Ask the children to discuss their observations and ask them if it's an illusion or real.

Painting with marbles
Using motion and movement to create art

What you need:
- Trays
- A4 white paper
- Marbles (different sizes)
- Food colouring or paint

What's in it for the children?
The children see motion and movement in action and use their communication skills to make predictions. They are also developing their expressive art and design skills by choosing colours and angling the trays so that the marbles make different patterns.

Taking it forward
- Ask the children to test out different-sized marbles and to hold the paper at different angles. Get them to make predictions about what might happen and why.
- Use the children's artwork to create a lovely wall display.

What to do:
1. Put a sheet of paper in the tray.
2. Ask the children to put a blob of food colouring or paint on the paper.
3. Ask the children to drop their marbles onto the food colouring or paint on the paper and tip their trays so that they are angled downwards. Discuss what happens when the marbles move.
4. Ask the children to repeat the previous step, using different colours to create patterns.

Top tip
Give each child at least three marbles of different sizes.

✚ Health & Safety
Carefully supervise young children when using marbles.

Hovercraft

Learning about how hovercraft work

What you need:
- Pictures or videos of hovercrafts
- Sticky tack
- Sports bottle lids (one per child)
- CDs (one per child)
- Balloons

What's in it for the children?
The children learn about the mechanism that a hovercraft uses and see the movement in action.

Taking it forward
- Ask the children to race their hovercrafts down the table or time them to see which hovercraft is the fastest.
- Film their hovercrafts and play it back in slow motion so the children can see the movement in more detail.

What to do:
1. Gather the children and ask them if they have seen a hovercraft before. Look at some pictures or videos of hovercrafts. Explain to them that hovercrafts are types of transport that use air to travel over water.
2. Explain to the children that they will be creating their own hovercraft with a balloon and CD.
3. Use the sticky tack to attach the closed bottle lid onto the hole of the CD, ensuring that the hole is not covered on the other side.
4. Pump up the balloon and put it over the lid without tying a knot over it.
5. Gently pull up the lid and watch the CD glide across the table on a cushion of air that is pushed out of the balloon.

Top tip
The activity works best with the lid from washing up liquid and sticky tack, but it also works with plasticine or play dough.

 Scan the QR code to see a video of this activity.

See-saw candle
Exploring balance and movement

What you need:
- Scissors
- A dinner candle (tall, non-tapered)
- A needle or pin (long)
- Two small drinking cups (identical size)
- Sticky tack or plasticine
- A table protector
- Matches or lighter

What to do:
1. Gather the children around the table and ask them what they know about see-saws. Show them the candle with the wick exposed at both ends and ask them how they might make a see-saw from it.
2. Stick the long needle through the middle of the candle, making a cross.
3. Balance the ends of the needle on two upturned drinking cups. Use the sticky tack to keep the ends in place.
4. Make sure that the table protector is under the candle to catch the wax.
5. Ask the children to watch what happens when you light the wick on either end of the candle.
6. Ask the children to observe the gentle see-saw movement as the wicks burn and each end gets heavy with wax.

Top tip
Before starting the activity, cut through the wax at both ends of the candle so that the wick is exposed. Practice the activity first before attempting with the children.

What's in it for the children?
This exciting activity will amaze young children and show them how weight can change the balance of a suspended object. They can relate it to prior knowledge about balance and see-saws.

Taking it forward
- Link this activity to learning about balance, for example by using scales (maths) or balancing on one foot (physical development).

Health & Safety
Supervise the children carefully around an open flame and ensure that they watch this activity from a safe distance.

Newton's theory of motion with coins
Motion in action

What you need:
- Glasses (one per child)
- Cardboard (one square per child)
- Coins (one per child)
- Sticky tack (optional)

What to do:
1. Gather the children and discuss who Isaac Newton was and how he developed several theories (see Newton's tumbling beads p.28). Explain that you will be showing them Newton's first law of motion.
2. Place a transparent glass on the table.
3. Put a square of cardboard over the top of a glass to cover it, then place a coin in middle of the cardboard.
4. Demonstrate that when you flick the side of the cardboard, the cardboard moves, but the coin remains in place for a nanosecond (less than a second) before gravity pulls the coin straight into the glass.
5. Let the children have a try and ask them to explain which object is moving and which object is stationary (staying still).

What's in it for the children?
The children will investigate Newton's first law of motion, which says that when an object is in motion it stays in motion and a stationary object stays stationary.

Taking it forward
- Fill the glass with water and ask the children if they think it will change the outcome of the experiment.
- Alternatively, ask the children to stack a few coins on the cardboard before flicking it and ask them to discuss their observations.

Top tip
Hold the glass down or use sticky tack to keep it in place so it doesn't fall when the children flick the cardboard.

 Scan the QR code to see a video of this activity.

Making a zip wire
Exploring the force of gravity

What you need:
- String
- Pipe cleaners
- Small LEGO® figure or any other small doll

What's in it for the children?
This fun and exciting activity helps the children learn about movement and gravity. Working together helps their communication and social skills and using characters encourages them to use their imaginations.

Taking it forward
- Get the children to test out different weighted objects and predict which ones will travel down their zip wires the fastest.
- Spark the children's imaginations by encouraging small world play in which their LEGO® characters use their zip wires.

What to do:
1. Gather the children and ask them if they know what a zip wire is. Explain to them that they are going to make their own zip wires.
2. Ask two children to take hold of the piece of string on either end, wrap the pipe cleaner around the LEGO® character or small doll and let it hang off the string.
3. Ask one child to lift one end of the string and ask the other child to lower the other end.
4. Ask the children to observe what happens to the LEGO® character. How quickly or slowly does it move and why?
5. Ask the children to use different lengths of string and different heights to observe which one gives the fastest results.

Top tip
Measure out different lengths of string to see which length works the best.

Scan the QR code to see a video of this activity.